George Eastman

History Maker Bios

Susan Bivin Aller

⌐ LERNER PUBLICATIONS COMPANY • MINNEAPOLIS

For Renate, who gives us truth and beauty through the lens of her camera

Illustrations by Tim Parlin

Text copyright © 2004 by Susan Bivin Aller
Illustrations copyright © 2004 by Lerner Publications Company

Lerner Publications Company
A division of Lerner Publishing Group
241 First Avenue North
Minneapolis, MN 55401 U.S.A.

Website address: www.lernerbooks.com

Library of Congress Cataloging-in-Publication Data

Aller, Susan Bivin.   .
      George Eastman / by Susan Bivin Aller.
          p.   cm. — (History maker bios)
      Summary: A biography of the man whose inventiveness and business savvy led to the creation of the Kodak company and transformed photography from a cumbersome professional activity to a point-and-click hobby enjoyed by people around the world.
      Includes bibliographical references and index.
      ISBN: 0–8225–0200–3 (lib. bdg. : alk. paper)
      1. Eastman, George, 1854–1932—Juvenile literature. 2. Photographic industry—United States—Biography—Juvenile literature. 3. Inventors—United States—Biography—Juvenile literature. [1. Eastman, George, 1854–1932. 2. Inventors. 3. Photography—History.] I. Title. II. Series.
TR140.E3 A43 2004
338.7'61681418'092—dc21   2002153397

Manufactured in the United States of America
1 2 3 4 5 6 – JR – 09 08 07 06 05 04

TABLE OF CONTENTS

INTRODUCTION

George Eastman fell in love with photography in 1877. At that time, cameras were expensive and difficult to use. Most photographers were professionals. They took pictures for a living. George was only an amateur, a person who does something he loves as a hobby. But he was also an inventor and a smart businessman. He figured there were many other people who would enjoy taking pictures as a hobby. If only it weren't so difficult.

George set about inventing film and cameras that were safe and easy to use. He even made a camera just for children. Soon people all over the world were taking photographs with George Eastman's cameras.

This is his story.

1 BORN TO MAKE MONEY

George Eastman was born on July 12, 1854, in Waterville, New York. He grew up in a house surrounded by roses and fruit trees. His father, George Washington Eastman, grew and sold plants. His mother, Maria Kilbourn Eastman, stayed home with baby George and his two older sisters, Ellen Maria and Emma Kate.

George's father taught his children to be responsible. Neighbors said that George's first time away from home was a trip to the bank. He went there in his baby carriage, pushed by his nine-year-old sister, Ellen. She was putting some money in the bank for their father. Mr. Eastman believed his children should be able to run errands by the age of five.

George at the age of three

George saw that his father was a smart and hardworking businessman. Along with his nursery, Mr. Eastman ran a successful business college with his brother in Rochester, New York. When George was six, Mr. Eastman sold the nursery business. He moved his family to Rochester.

In 1862, George's father died unexpectedly. He left behind a widow and three young children.

George's father, George Washington Eastman, was a talented businessman.

EARLY PHOTOGRAPHY

When George was a boy, photography was a new idea. People did not own cameras. They paid trained photographers to take their picture. Traveling photographers came through George's town. People could also go to studios to have their portraits taken. But George's family must not have been very interested in this new invention. Only a few early Eastman family photographs survive.

George's mother needed to bring in money for the family. She did what many widows had to do in such cases. She rented out rooms in her house to boarders. Luckily, there was enough money to send George to a good private school.

Like his father, George believed in the importance of education. But he wanted to help pay household bills. At the age of thirteen, George decided to leave school and work instead. It was his own decision. His mother did not approve.

Young George was determined to make something of himself.

George worked full-time as an office boy in an insurance company. He was as ambitious and hardworking as his father had been. George liked to tackle problems at his job. He could almost always solve them. His boss noticed his hard work.

To improve himself, he took classes to learn accounting and French. But he also knew how to have fun.

In his account book, George carefully recorded expenses for dancing lessons, a fishing pole, and two flutes. He bought tickets to lectures and joined a fitness gym. He also loved to travel. Once he spent more than three weeks' pay on a trip to New York City.

George kept a detailed list of all his earnings and expenses. He was glad when he had saved enough money to give some to his mother.

George saved money as well as he earned it.

By the age of nineteen, George was assistant bookkeeper at the Rochester Savings Bank. His salary was three times what many people earned. But George wasn't satisfied. He added to his savings by working nights as a Rochester fireman. He also made money by buying land to sell later to builders.

By the time he was twenty-one, George was riding high on his success. He and his mother moved into a better house. He bought gifts for himself and his family. He even made a donation to a stranger in need. He gave one dollar to an injured boy.

2 A PACKHORSE LOAD

At the age of twenty-three, George had a lot of energy and ambition. He wanted to be something more than a banker. But what? He decided to invest in some land in the Caribbean. He thought it would be a good idea to go there and take pictures of it.

George bought a camera and other things he needed. It was "a pack-horse load," he said. The camera was large. It had to sit on a stand called a tripod. He also needed to buy chemicals and a black darkroom tent for making photographs.

Taking pictures was very complicated in the 1870s. Only professional photographers knew how to do it. George paid a photographer to give him lessons.

George took this photograph, his first one, in the fall of 1877.

A photographer needed a lot of equipment in the 1870s.

George practiced using his camera outdoors. He set up his darkroom tent and went in with his equipment. Inside, he coated a thick glass plate with egg white and chemicals. After that he dipped the plate into another chemical mixture that made the plate sensitive to light.

While the plate was still wet, he put it into the camera. He aimed the camera at his subject and took the picture. Then he had to take the glass plate out of the camera before it dried.

PEDAL POWER

George loved to ride a bicycle. His first one had a high front wheel and a small back wheel. He rode it to the bank every day. Even after George had a chauffeur to drive him places, he rode his bicycle to work on nice days. He parked it in the basement of his office building.

Inside the darkroom tent, he dipped the plate in a tank of liquid chemicals to make a photographic negative. The negative could be used later to make a photograph.

It was a lot of work. But George was thrilled to be able to take pictures himself. He called photography "the most fascinating amusement."

George never visited the Caribbean to buy land there. Instead he stayed at the bank. He spent his free time thinking of ways to make photography easier. He could sell cameras and glass plates to amateurs like himself. He saw a bright future for himself in the photography business.

Messy wet plates were difficult for an amateur to handle. George studied the problem. He discovered that British photographers had found a way to coat glass plates with a new mixture called gelatin emulsion.

The emulsion was sensitive to light even after it dried. That meant a photographer could carry a supply of dry plates with him. And after he took his pictures, he could take them back to a darkroom to turn into photographs. He didn't have to carry liquid chemicals with him.

A glass plate was dipped in chemicals to make it sensitive to light. George made dry plates that were ready to use.

Employees at the Rochester Savings Bank. George is in the front row, (FAR LEFT).

George saw that this was a real breakthrough. He dropped everything but his bank job to work on making his own dry plates. He no longer had time for friends and amusements. He worked all day at the bank. Then he went home and cooked up batches of emulsion in the kitchen. He often worked all night. His mother would find him asleep on the floor in the morning.

George finally succeeded in making the gelatin emulsion. But it was hard to spread the mixture evenly on glass plates. He invented a coating machine that did it better.

Here was something the British dry-plate companies might buy from him. So George went to England. There he patented his invention. The patent said that no one could copy his idea without his permission. Then George talked to London dry-plate companies about his invention. They were interested in paying him for the right to use his machine. When George returned to Rochester, he had grand plans for starting his own business.

In London, George spent most of his time trying to sell his new products.

In April 1880, he rented a large room above a music store in downtown Rochester. He turned the room into a factory and began making dry plates. He planned to sell the dry plates directly to photographers.

Every day, George rode his bicycle to work with his lunch in a shoe box strapped to the back. At three, the bank closed. Then George went to his one-room factory and worked all night. He took short naps in a hammock.

George hoped to make a fortune from his inventions.

A package of George's dry plates

George did all the work himself. He mixed emulsion and coated plates. He sold the coated dry plates, and he did the bookkeeping. The factory was neat and efficient, just like George.

Slowly George's business grew. Studio photographers were slow to change from wet to dry plates. They thought pictures made from wet plates were better. But amateur photographers liked the easier dry-plate method. They weren't so critical of the quality. George sold his products to more and more customers.

By the end of 1880, George had made a good profit. He hired six employees and looked for a larger space for his factory. He also looked for someone to invest money in his business. He found that someone in Henry Alvah Strong.

Strong was a wealthy businessman who had once boarded at the Eastman's house. Strong thought George was a genius. He invested several thousand dollars and became George's partner. The new Eastman Dry Plate Company opened on January 1, 1881.

3 YOU PRESS THE BUTTON . . .

he time had come for George to put all of his energy into his new business. He quit his job at the bank. He bought land to build a modern factory. Then he ran into a big problem.

Customers had begun complaining. They said the newest Eastman dry plates were not working properly. George immediately stopped making dry plates and bought back the bad ones. He had to find a solution to the problem, or he would lose everything.

He tried 469 different ways to make the gelatin emulsion. Nothing worked. Finally he sailed to London to see the man who sold him his gelatin. After spending a week there, he discovered the reason for the problem. One of the ingredients—gelatin— was at fault.

George's first business partner, Henry Strong

Who would have guessed that cows were to blame for the failure of George's dry plates?

Even though gelatin was always made from the bones and skins of cattle, it wasn't all the same. The quality of gelatin depended on what kind of grass and seeds the cattle ate. His gelatin seller was getting gelatin from a different place, and it didn't make good emulsion. George insisted on the original gelatin, and that solved the problem.

George needed new products to keep his company growing. Dry plates were better than wet plates. But amateur photographers still found them difficult to handle. They were heavy and breakable. George wanted to change that.

By 1884, he had come up with an entirely new invention. He succeeded in making long strips of paper coated with a special gelatin. He called his invention "American Film." The film was rolled onto a spool and placed in a holder. The holder attached to the back of a camera in the same way a glass plate holder attached.

George tested his new film by taking a photo of himself in 1884.

George's film was much lighter than glass plates. It wouldn't break the way glass did. But the camera was still big and heavy.

Over the next few years, George worked on this problem. He designed a small, lightweight box camera for his roll film. The camera was just 6¾ inches long and weighed less than 2 pounds. In 1888, he patented his new product. He called it a Kodak camera. George had invented the word *Kodak*. He thought it would be catchy and easy to remember.

George took the camera to a large meeting of photographers in the United States. The Kodak camera caused a sensation. It was inexpensive and easier to use than any other camera. For $25, people got the camera, leather carrying case, shoulder strap, and an instruction book.

NAMING THE KODAK

George told different stories about how he came up with the Kodak name. In one story, he said he made up the name while playing a word game with his mother. He moved the letters of the game around on the table and made the word *Kodak*. He told someone else that he found the word *Kodak* floating in a bowl of alphabet soup! At any rate, it was the perfect name for his camera.

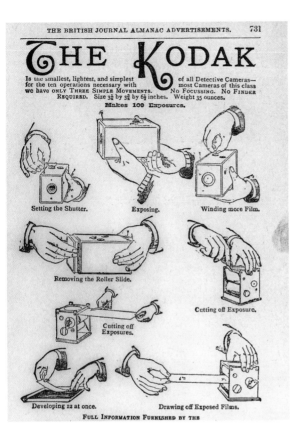

THE KODAK

Is the smallest, lightest, and simplest of all Detective Cameras— for the ten operations necessary with most Cameras of this class we have ONLY THREE SIMPLE MOVEMENTS. No FOCUSSING. No FINDER REQUIRED. Size 3¼ by 3¾ by 6½ inches. Weight 35 ounces.

Makes 100 Exposures.

Setting the Shutter.

Exposing.

Winding more Film.

Removing the Roller Slide.

Cutting off Exposure.

Cutting off Exposures.

Developing 12 at once.

Drawing off Exposed Films.

FULL INFORMATION FURNISHED BY THE

The Kodak camera could be used in eight easy steps.

George knew that photography was not just about using a camera. Photographers also had to turn the film into photographs, or prints. There were some people who wanted to learn the skills needed to do both. But George sensed many, many more people just wanted to take a picture. Let somebody else take the film and make prints from it.

George Eastman took pictures with a Kodak camera on a ship in 1890.

He had the idea to sell his Kodak camera with a roll of film already inside. It was long enough for one hundred pictures. When all the film had been used, the "Kodaker" sent the camera back to the Eastman Company. Employees opened the camera and made prints from the film. Then they sent the prints and camera—loaded with a new roll of film—back to the owner.

George's idea changed photography forever. He wrote an advertising slogan that said it all: "You press the button. We do the rest."

Orders poured in. George's company could hardly keep up with them. Five thousand Kodak cameras were sold in the first six months.

The Eastman Company kept ahead of everybody else in the quality of its film and photographic paper. Cameras made by other companies might be as good as or better than Kodak's. But people needed only one camera. It was the printing paper and film they replaced again and again.

"You·press·the·button
We·do·the·rest"

Advertisements used the famous Kodak slogan to sell cameras.

Of course, there were other companies that tried to cut in on George's business. But George was a skilled businessman. He hired trained chemists and engineers to develop new and better products. He had machinery to make cameras and film cheaply. And he protected everything he made by patents.

George also knew how to attract customers from all over the globe. Advertising was the key to reaching them.

The Eastman factory and office building

George had a talent for making good ads. One magazine ad took advantage of another popular hobby, riding bicycles. The ad showed a man on a bicycle. He was steering with one hand and holding his Kodak with the other.

In 1900, George had another brilliant idea. He made a small camera called the Kodak Brownie just for children. The Brownie cost one dollar. A roll of film cost fifteen cents. George even set up the Brownie Camera Club. Children who joined the club could enter photography contests. His new product was an immediate success. Thousands of Kodak Brownies sold within the first few months.

4 KODAK AROUND THE WORLD

The name Kodak had become famous
around the world. Even the
president of the United States, Grover
Cleveland, had a Kodak camera. He took it
with him on a hunting trip.

By 1901, George's company was called the Eastman Kodak Company. Every morning he bounded up the stairs to his office two at a time. He was always eager to begin the day. Employees greeted him with a polite "Good morning, Mr. Eastman." Privately, they called him "G.E."

The survival of George's company was his main goal. He fired disloyal employees, and he sued people who stole his ideas. He controlled what his salesmen did and how his dealers sold Kodak products. He even wrote the instructions for his cameras himself.

George expected his employees to work hard. But he treated them well.

George also knew that his employees were an important part of his success. They would be loyal and produce better work if he took good care of them. He did more than just pay his workers well. He also gave them a share of the company's profits. And he helped them save money for later in life. Many workers have come to expect this kind of treatment. But in the 1900s, it was unheard of.

THE GEORGE EASTMAN HOUSE

In 1905, George built the largest private house in Rochester. It had more than fifty rooms. He surrounded the house with gardens for flowers, fruits, and vegetables. An orchard and a grape arbor grew on the property. He had barns for horses and cows and buildings for carriages and cars. Inside the house was a large pipe organ. Every morning, George ate breakfast to music played for him by his own organist.

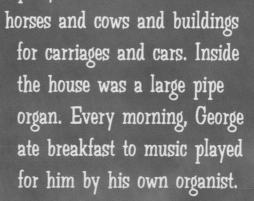

On a trip to Africa, George (RIGHT) carefully organized the camping equipment and did most of the cooking for his friends.

George still spent long hours at work. But it was important for him to balance work with travel and other activities. He liked to spend time at his vacation home in North Carolina. Oak Lodge was surrounded by forests and farmland. There he relaxed with friends and enjoyed being outdoors.

George started taking long trips several times a year. He and a group of friends traveled by train across the United States and by bicycle through Europe.

George's love of adventure took him to places few American tourists had ever been, including Russia. He even went on several safaris in Africa.

Happily, he found that his business did not fall apart when he took a vacation. By the early 1900s, the Eastman Kodak Company was Rochester's largest employer. And George Eastman was its wealthiest citizen.

5 GIVING IT ALL AWAY

George Eastman wanted to do something good with his wealth. He had begun giving small amounts of money as a young man. In his 50s, he decided to give away large parts of his fortune.

Many people in his position kept all of their money. Their wealth was given to others after they died. George was different. He liked to control his money and his life. He wanted to be alive to see the results of his gifts.

He began at home, in the city of Rochester. It was a practical decision. He wanted to make Rochester a better city to live in. Then he could attract the most skilled employees for his Kodak Company.

George sits in front of a portrait of himself as a successful businessman.

George donated money for the Eastman Theatre in Rochester.

George also considered Rochester to be his hometown. He had no children to give his money to. In a way, the people of Rochester were like his children. He gave money to hospitals, schools, colleges, theaters, and a symphony orchestra. He made the whole city of Rochester bloom by giving money for new parks.

Another of George's special interests was dental care for children. As a boy, he had had serious problems with his teeth. There was no good dental care for most people in those days. He wanted to save poor children in Rochester from the same kind of problems he had suffered.

Privately Generous

George often kept his own name a secret when he gave a large gift. He didn't want to be in the spotlight. The largest secret gift he made was to the Massachusetts Institute of Technology, or MIT. Some of his company's best scientists had studied at this university. He was impressed by the school. Over many years, a Mr. Smith gave $20 million to MIT. Finally people learned that Mr. Smith was really George Eastman!

George built dental clinics where poor children could be treated for all kinds of tooth and mouth problems. It cost their parents only five cents a visit. Later, George paid for dental clinics in European cities where Kodak had employees.

George believed in education for all people. He gave some of his largest gifts to two colleges for African American students. The schools were Tuskegee Normal and Industrial Institute in Alabama and Hampton Institute in Virginia.

George Eastman died in 1932, at the age of 77. By then he had given away more than 100 million dollars. These gifts helped make life healthier, more beautiful, and more fulfilling for millions of people.

George Eastman had fallen in love with photography at the age of twenty-three. Back then, it took a packhorse load of equipment to make pictures. Fifty years later, the whole world could just "press the button."

George Eastman had done the rest.

TIMELINE

In the year . . .

1860	George moved with his family to Rochester, New York. **Age 6**
1862	his father died.
1868	he quit school and began working for an insurance company.
1877	he bought his first camera.
1878	he invented a dry-plate coating machine. **Age 23**
1880	he set up a dry-plate factory in a room above a music store.
1881	he formed the Eastman Dry Plate Company with Henry Alvah Strong on January 1. **Age 26**
1882	his company moved to a large factory on 343 State Street in Rochester.
1885	he invented rolled paper "American Film."
1888	he invented the first Kodak camera.
1897	he bought land in North Carolina for his Oak Lodge retreat. **Age 43**
1900	he invented the Kodak Brownie.
1905	he moved into his new mansion in Rochester, later known as the George Eastman House.
1917	his dental clinic for poor families opened in Rochester.
1919	it was revealed that he had given more than 20 million dollars to MIT under the name Mr. Smith.
1932	he died on March 14. **Age 77**

INVENTING A NEW WORLD

George lived in a time of great change. In the twenty-seven years between 1876 and 1903, many amazing inventions came into being. George Eastman's work played an important part in this leap toward our modern world. Here are some other important modern inventions:

1876 telephone
1877 phonograph (early sound recorder)
1879 modern electric lightbulb
      cash register
1885 photographic film
      gasoline-powered automobile
1886 dishwasher
1891 motion picture machine
1892 escalator
1893 zipper
1895 X-ray machine
      wireless radio
1901 vacuum cleaner
1902 modern air conditioner
1903 airplane

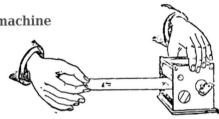

FURTHER READING

NONFICTION

Gaines, Ann Graham. *American Photographers: Capturing the Image.* **Berkeley Heights, NJ: Enslow Publishers, Inc., 2002.** A collection of biographies on America's greatest photographers.

Gibbon, Gail. *Click! A Book about Cameras and Taking Pictures.* **Boston: Little, Brown & Co., 1997.** An illustrated exploration of a camera's parts and the process of taking photographs.

Jeunesse, Gallimard, Claude Delafosse and Pierre-Marie Valat, eds. *The Camera: Snapshots, Movies, Videos, and Cartoons.* **New York: Scholastic, 1993.** Using illustrated transparencies, this book explores the insides of a camera, photographic development, the process of cartoon animation, and other film-related topics.

Johnson, Neil. *National Geographic Photography Guide for Kids.* **Washington, D.C.: National Geographic Society, 2001.** A how-to guide for the young camera enthusiast.

FICTION

Castle, Caroline. *Grandpa Baxter and the Photographs.* **New York: Orchard Books, 1993.** A teddy bear named Benjamin learns about his family's history when he looks through a photo album with his grandfather.

Conford, Ellen. *Get the Picture, Jenny Archer?* **Boston: Little, Brown & Co., 1994.** In this charming chapter book, Jenny Archer signs up for a photography contest and gets into trouble taking candid pictures of her friends and neighbors.

WEBSITES

George Eastman House
<www.eastman.org>
The official website of the George Eastman House and the International Museum of Photography and Film.

The Kodak Company's Official Website
<www.kodak.com/US/en/corp/aboutKodak/kodakHistory/kodakHistory.shtml>
Include links to the company's history and the life of its founder, George Eastman.

The Smithsonian Institute: Inventors and Innovations
<www.si.edu/resource/faq/nmah/invent.htm>
This website includes information on famous inventors and inventions.

SELECT BIBLIOGRAPHY

Ackerman, Carl W. *George Eastman.* Boston: Houghton Mifflin, 1930.

Brayer, Elizabeth. *George Eastman.* Baltimore: The Johns Hopkins University Press, 1996.

Jenkins, Reese V. *Images and Enterprise: Technology and the American Photographic Industry, 1839–1925.* Baltimore: The Johns Hopkins University Press, 1975.

Newhall, Beaumont. *The History of Photography from 1839 to the Present Day.* New York: Museum of Modern Art, 1964.

Solbert, Oscar N. *George Eastman.* Rochester: The George Eastman House, Inc., 1953.

INDEX

Acknowledgements

For photographs and artwork: © Hulton-Deutsch Collection/CORBIS, p. 4; © George Eastman House, pp. 7, 8, 10, 14, 15, 17, 18, 21, 24, 26, 27, 29, 41, 45; © PhotoDisc Royalty Free, p. 11; © Library of Congress LC-DIG-ppmsc-08576, p. 19; © Todd Strand/Independent Picture Service, p. 20; © Agricultural Research Service, USDA, p. 25; © Bettmann/CORBIS, pp. 31, 37; © Hulton Archive/Getty Images, pp. 30, 32, 40; © Underwood & Underwood/CORBIS, p. 35. Front cover © George Eastman House; Back cover © Paul Almasy/CORBIS.